THE ATHLETE'S

MEDIA PLAYBOOK

Jill Schiefelbein

Copyright © 2013 by Impromptu Guru
All rights reserved. Printed in the United States of America. This publication is protected by Copyright and permission should be obtained from the publisher prior to any prohibited reproduction, storage in a retrieval system, or transmission in any form or by any means, electronic, mechanical, photocopying, recording, or likewise.

For information regarding permission(s), write to:

Impromptu Guru, LLC
P.O. Box 392
Higley, AZ 85036

To every athlete,

May you always remember that you have the capacity to impact a child's life.

Use this power wisely.

Table of Contents

Introduction

> Chapter 1
> Reality: Face it

Part 1: The Rules of the Game

> Chapter 2
> Media: Friend or foe?
>
> Chapter 3
> Sticks and Stones: Words CAN and DO hurt
>
> Chapter 4
> Simon Says: Actions DO speak louder than words
>
> Chapter 5
> Building Relationships: Hug with words

Part 2: Learning the Plays

> Chapter 6
> Pick-Up Lines: Interview responses that won't get you turned down
>
> Chapter 7
> Trash Talk: What NOT to say to a reporter
>
> Chapter 8
> Bad Breath: What to do when reporters get too close or comfortable

Table of Contents

Part 2: Learning the Plays, continued

Chapter 9
Execution: Delivery matters

Part 3: Onward to Victory

Chapter 10
Overtime: Win after the interview and build community

Chapter 11
Death by Twitter: Social media mistakes to avoid

Conclusion

Chapter 12
Beyond the Game: Your next steps

Introduction

Chapter 1

Reality: Face it

You've made it. You have the contract. You have the signing bonus. Or you're working hard as heck to get that big break. Whatever the case, if you're an athlete with pro aspirations, there are some cold hard facts that you need to understand if you care about your earning potential during and after your days on the field.

The media is a big part of that.

Many of you may have mixed feelings about the media, or have a few choice words to say about some interview experiences that you've had. I get it. Bad media does exist. I won't sugar coat it. But as the center of attention, you have the power to have the media eating out of the palm of your hand.

Really.

You have the power to not answer a question. You have the choice to deny an interview. And you have the choice to decide that you're going to make the media your new best friend and leverage the heck out of it to make your career soar on and off the court.

There are game statistics and there are media statistics. The combination of both will allow you to gain star power that will outlast your playing time.

But most media training that my clients have told me about is pretty (1) boring, (2) intimidating, (3) useless or (4) limiting. I had one client tell me that all the trainer did was talk to them about what NOT to say. Talk about the wrong approach!

Yes, there are some topics that should be avoided, but what about YOU? What about who YOU are? Who YOU want to represent?

I take a different approach.

I teach you how to kick a** and take names. You'll make mistakes. But you'll also learn how to recover from them. If you don't make mistakes, you're not trying hard enough. The key is not making a mistake that will take you out of the game — put you on the injured reserve list so to speak.

This book will tell you how.

My goal is to get you to (1) understand the media landscape and the reality of what the media can do FOR and WITH you, (2) learn some basic skills that will help with the day-to-day interviews that you'll likely encounter, and (3) gain some tips for how to see yourself as a part of a bigger society where you have unlimited potential to make a positive impact.

Together, in this book, we'll discover speaking tips that can make you stand out. We'll talk about ways to handle tough questions and we'll look at examples. Together we'll flesh out techniques that you can use to get the media on your side. And we'll even talk a little bit about social media.

As a communication and media coach who works with athletes at different levels of collegiate and professional play, and who communicates with the media professionals who work with these athletes, I'll give you the inside scoop.

The beauty of being part of a team is that you are surrounded by people who want you to succeed. Every coach and team president I've worked with genuinely wants athletes to succeed in every capacity.

And I love working with people who are focused on success.

Here's your first tip — Develop relationships. Getting to know people and letting people get to know you is key to advancing your career. They don't teach this in high school or college. Or they may mention it, but they don't tell you how to do it.

Since we're going to be spending 12 chapters together, let's get to know each other a little better.

Let me tell you a story.

It's in the middle of the worst season in the WNBA Phoenix Mercury's history. Injuries have plagued the roster and the 6th, 7th, 8th, 9th and 10th bench players are asked to step up.

More time on the court means more time in the spotlight for players who aren't used to significant media attention. I'm asked to help.

I go to meet my first victim. I joke — but most athletes don't get too excited about seeing a communication and media coach. I get it. I'm real. And I'm not offended. If I were in your shoes, with people "offering" to help me left and right and not knowing if someone is being genuine or just trying to make a buck off of you, I'd probably be a little unsure too.

It's August 2012. I'm sitting in the officials' locker room at US Airways Center in Phoenix, Arizona. In walks a 6' 4" forward, fierce as heck on the court, but looking like a deer in headlights. I'm working with DeWanna Bonner, the WNBA's 6th woman of the year for 3 years in a row. And she's now in the starting lineup.

I introduce myself. We sit. Her posture is standoffish. Not in a mean way, but in an "I don't want to be here but maybe I should" way.

My advice — check the ego at the door. Nobody gets to the top level in anything — sport or business — without the help of a coach. In this case, I'm just another coach.

I ask her, as I do many of my clients when I first meet them, "Why do you love being interviewed?" She looks at me like I'm crazy. I smile and laugh. She relaxes. And we go on to have a very productive and beneficial hour together. The buzzer sounds and our session ends. The woman who walked in the room tentative and skeptical stands up and embraces me in a big hug.

> "This wasn't anything like I thought it would be," she said. "Thank you so much."

This is why I do what I do. Even in just one hour, I know I can make an impact.

I can give someone the tools he or she needs to be more confident and more comfortable during a future interview. Which could snowball into more media appearances, which will inspire a girl or boy somewhere watching, which will increase the respect for the game, which is good for everyone involved.

Get it?

You're part of not only a team, but a whole culture of sport that has the power to influence billions.

Being interviewed on camera probably wasn't your first priority when you started playing your sport. You may never love speaking to an audience as much as I do. But when I can get someone to feel a little more confident, a little more comfortable and even a little more proud of herself, I've made a difference.

I'm a small-town Kansas girl at heart, who grew up a tomboy, playing every sport she could get involved in. My mom wanted me to play with dolls. I wanted to roll around, get dirty, tackle, box out, shoot, run, hit or do anything that the boys did. And that did include playing with dolls of some sort—but we called them action figures.

As an adult, I still play, just not on the big screen. I had some knee injuries in high school and went a different path. Besides, I'm 5'9" and was a forward by small-town Kansas standards. And although my shooting percentage was pretty darn good, my dribbling skills were severely lacking. I won't lie. So the kneecap dislocating and the bones grinding into one another was a sign.

I took it.

Instead I did the leadership thing. I did the academic thing. I did the computer thing. And I did the motivational speaking thing. I'm one of those people who got a full ride that didn't play sports. Some might call me a nerd. Go right ahead.

I own my geekness. I own my brand. And I do it with confidence.

I still believe in staying active, and I cycle and occasionally compete in triathlons. I've done an Ironman. I've "escaped" from Alcatraz, swimming to shore after hopping off a ferry in cold as you-know-what, choppy waters.

I've battled health issues and injuries and a couple near-death experiences. I've succeeded and I've had fear. I know what it's like to cross a finish line. And I know what it's like to win.

I also know what it's like to put everything that you have into something and have it not go as planned. The last thing you want to do is have someone from the crowd come up to you and ask you questions. You're physically, mentally and emotionally drained. Can't I just have some "me" time?

The reality is, not right away — not if you want to build your image, your brand, your reputation and your earning potential.

I get it. It may not be on a court or field, but after I give a big keynote presentation that I put my heart and soul into (and I get worked up — I'm moving around, sweating, but putting my all into it) the LAST thing I want to do is plaster a smile on my face and shake hands with dozens, if not hundreds, of people in the audience.

But if I don't, my reputation suffers.

My speaker's fee won't be as high. And I won't build the connections that people REALLY want from those they admire and those who inspire them. My brand, my image, my earning potential are all on the line each and every time I grab that microphone.

The same goes for you with every media encounter.

It's reality. And, yes, it may bite. But let me tell you, you can leverage the heck out of it so that you get the media to work not only WITH you, but FOR you.

Sound good?

The warm up is done.

It's game time.

Part 1:
The Rules of the Game

Now that you know where I'm coming from, and you know that the media can help you expand your career beyond the arena, let me give you some information that will set you apart from the competition.

There are unspoken and unwritten rules for working with the media. Lucky for you, they're presented in this book! Use these rules to better understand the media landscape, and to help you advance your career.

Chapter 2

Media: Friend or foe?

It's up to you.

The media can be your best friend, or your worst nightmare. Yes, many athletes feel that the media are "out to get them" but, let's be real, in many situations that athlete has done something to draw the negative attention his or her way. And negative or juicy stories sell. Some networks or outlets are drawn to that more than others.

But you know what else sells? Inspiration. Hopes. Dreams. Keeping it Real. (I'm not talking about Dave Chappelle's "When Keeping it Real Goes Wrong" here...I'm talking about being open and honest and telling your story — we'll go into that more later).

And you can sell these each and every time you get approached by a reporter.

If you want to make the media your friend, and build a connection with reporters that will keep you in the positive light during and after your career, here are some things that you need to do.

I'll break each one down for you simply. These are just the basics. We'll get into what you do and say DURING your interviews in later chapters.

Your momma was right: Say please and thank you

It's simple, right? But how many people forget to do it? Or don't do it proactively? A ton. And it's sad. Can you imagine changing the script on a reporter?

What would it be like if, before a reporter asks you a single question, you say:

> "Thank you for letting me share with your audience."

I guarantee you that many have never heard a proactive, pre-interview thank-you before.

The after-interview words of thanks are much more common, but you shouldn't forget! Yes, you are helping the reporter by giving him sound bites for a story, but he is also helping you by putting YOUR face and words out there. So thank them for that! You'll be surprised at the difference it can make once you do it consistently.

Ask not what a reporter can do for you,
but what you can do for a reporter

After the interview reaches its end, ask:

> "Is there anything else that I may talk about or answer that will help with your story?"

Doing this during a live interview while the camera is rolling probably isn't the best strategy. But as you're shaking hands to part ways, ask!

If a reporter knows you are willing to work WITH him, you're more likely to get requested for interviews in the future. And, who knows, you might get an additional feature right on the spot! This also shows that you respect what the reporter is doing as a profession. And that never hurts!

Reciprocity: Share the love

If a reporter does a special story about you and puts it out via social media and "tags" or "tweets" you in any way, SHARE IT with your followers and fans. This simple click will endear you to reporters near and far, as they will realize that you're conscious of what is put out about you in the media and that you're also happy to share their work.

Think of it this way: If you break a single-game record and tweet it out on your account, don't you feel good when you see people replying, retweeting, favoriting or sharing in some way? I bet so! Reporters are people too. This will go a long way toward developing relationships.

Your Game Plan

- Say **THANK YOU** before and after an interview.
- **ASK** what you can do to help the reporter.
- **SHARE** the work that others produce or publish about you.

Chapter 3

Sticks and Stones:
Words CAN and DO hurt

Ever say something that you wish you could take back? Most of us have. When you're in the limelight, your words are magnified even more.

That's why any slight of tongue can get you in trouble and hurt not only your own reputation, but the reputation of your team or organization as well. And it's not just saying something politically incorrect or taboo that can get you in trouble. You can also get a negative image by speaking poorly and/or acting a fool.

Let's be honest. Many athletes don't have a reputation for being the most well-spoken or composed during interviews. That's why, if you can even make small gains in this area, you'll be miles ahead of the rest.

As I mentioned earlier, this can help not only your reputation, but it will also make you more valuable to the organization and put you in the position to gain more high-paying endorsements.

How do you make sure your words don't hurt? Here are three ways.

Know your surroundings

The world is a stage, and you're a constant performer. With technology so easily accessible, anyone can be standing behind you with a camera phone ready to record your every word or slip up.

Think you're having a private party with friends? Unless you can trust them all 100% you can't put anyone on blast or throw out slang that would be offensive to others, especially your teammates!

Is this fair? It doesn't matter. It's reality. If you don't want your words to hurt you, your team, and your chances for a successful career, you need to pay attention to your surroundings, and know when you're in a place where you can speak freely, and when you're in a place where you might need to be more guarded. It's not ideal. I'm just keeping it real.

St st st stop stuttering

First, if you've never seen a video of, or listened to, yourself giving an interview, you need to do so immediately.

Put down this book now and do it.

Was it painful to watch? Was it okay? How did you feel? Did you see areas for improvement but don't know how to improve?

(*Good thing you have this book.*)

We are our own worst critics. But in this day and age if you stutter or sound like an idiot in an interview, it's instantly all over the media, Twitter, Facebook, and YouTube — your inarticulateness in all its glory.

If you have the tendency to stutter or use filler words (um, uh, so, like, hmmm, etc.) you need to learn to do one thing.

Pause.

Yes, it's that simple.

You do not need to be uttering sound the entire time during an interview. A pause can be purposeful, strategic and helpful. A pause will keep you from spitting out those words that have no purpose.

Let's take a look at an interview transcript in its unedited splendor.

> Reporter: What does this season look like for Team XYZ?
>
> Athlete: Well, man, it's uh going to be great, man, and I'm uh ready to get started. We have, you know, a lot of talent on our team, man, and uh, it's going to be fun, uh, to see where it goes, man.

Now, let's look at this without filler words.

> Reporter: What does this season look like for Team XYZ?

> Athlete: It's going to be great. I'm ready to get started. We have a lot of talent on our team, and it's going to be fun to see where it goes.

Notice the difference? So does everyone else.

Repeat the question

Are you exhausted at halftime or after the game? Is the last thing you want to think about the loss your team just had? Are you already celebrating in your head but need to keep it together?

All of these things are normal. There's a trick to making an interview easier no matter what the situation may be.

Repeating the question.

I'm not talking word-for-word, but if you paraphrase the question back to the reporter, you give yourself some time to think about your response, take a breath, and answer intelligently.

Here's an example:

> Reporter: What do you think your team can learn from tonight's loss?

Athlete: I think we can learn a lot from tonight's loss. (*Buying some time and sounding great from the start.*) We worked hard, but it wasn't enough. The other team played really well. We'll watch some film and learn from the experience.

Notice how in that response there wasn't a specific answer, but yet you sound well composed and respectful of the other team's talent. Now that's a response that will get a repeat interview! And if the reporter wants a more specific answer, you've opened the door for her to ask another question.

YOUR GAME PLAN

- **BE AWARE** of your surroundings.
- **PAUSE** instead of stuttering or using fillers.
- **REPEAT** the question to compose your response.

Chapter 4

Simon Says:
Actions DO speak louder than words

I don't know anyone who's perfect. Nor do I want to. We all slip up. We all make mistakes. That makes us human.

But as an athlete your mistakes have the potential to make the nightly news. It's important to know this: Actions speak louder than words.

Sure, your mom probably told you this when you were younger. It's the truth.

If you are gracious and kind in your interviews and then go start a fight at a bar, what do you think is going to be remembered?

Your action.

No question.

In the same respect, if you just do okay during an interview, but then go spend time volunteering in the community, that action will go further than your words.

It can go both ways. Use it for your benefit.

Match: Make your actions and words synonymous

If you want to get the maximum benefit and exposure for yourself as an athlete and for your team, you want to make sure that your actions and your words match—and match in a positive way.

If you don't demonstrate good sportsmanship on the field but then try to put it forward in an interview, people will remember your actions on the field more than the words you say.

Play hard, play well, and if you make a mistake on the field, admit it in the interview, apologize, and get it out of the way. Then you're consistent, you're honest, and you'll have people ready to pay attention. Here's an example.

Reporter: You were pretty fired up out there tonight. Do you have anything to say about the four penalties that were assessed?

Athlete: You're right.

(Don't try to play it off or deny it. Everyone saw it.)

Sometimes I get so wound up in the game that the emotions drive me, and not always for the better. I have nothing but respect for our opponent, and my passion for the game came out in a negative way. I know I need to work on that.

Isn't that good? The reporter tried to lead with a question and the athlete owned his actions right away. This leads to trust. This demonstrates honesty. And this will get you more favorable reviews.

Follow-through

This is simple. If you say you're going to do something, do it. We are all familiar with those who are all talk and no action. Don't be that person.

It's just like being that player that cocks off and talks smack before a game and then doesn't show up to play. Nobody likes that person. Nobody will rely on that person. And in many cases the teammates will get annoyed, or worse, at that person. (Not to mention coaches, fans, scouts, agents…you get the idea.)

If a coach tells you to run a play and you don't execute, you get benched (or at the very least reprimanded). When you don't follow through, there are repercussions.

The same goes with the media.

If you say you'll give an interview and then don't, or try to rush through it, your actions speak louder than your words and you are going to be viewed as someone who doesn't keep her promises. And you don't want to move the media out of your corner.

Don't get benched by the media. Your career can't afford it.

Show Respect: Nonverbals are actions too

Ever try to pick someone up (in a flirting sense) who just wasn't feeling you? Her nonverbal behaviors were probably loud and clear. And she didn't have to say a word.

Nonverbal behaviors are also actions.

When you're giving an interview, your body language communicates just as much as, if not more than, your words.

You want to make sure that your body language matches your message, and demonstrates that you are engaged in the interview. But how do you ensure this?

Here are a few tips.

Make eye contact with the reporter
It doesn't have to be continual, but it should be like you're having a conversation. Pay attention. This person is someone who can help elevate your career.

Stand up straight
You don't have to have perfect posture, but show up. Don't slouch. Respect that you are present to give an interview, and that the reporter has a job to do.

You wouldn't like it if your coach only paid half attention to you. Don't do that to anyone else.

Get your voice into it
It's okay to get a little excitement in your voice. It's okay to show a little disappointment with your tone. Have some variation.

Be a real person. That's who people relate to. And that's what people will believe.

YOUR GAME PLAN

- Make sure your actions and words **MATCH**.
- Always **FOLLOW-THROUGH** and keep promises that you make.
- Show **RESPECT** through appropriate body language.

Chapter 5

Relationships: Hug with words

Often athletes are told to stick to a script. And on one hand I understand the reason universities, professional teams, and organizations do this — to keep a consistent image and message. But on the other hand, I would never want to be kept to a script.

A script has the tendency to make athletes feel constrained and restricted. A script also has the tendency to come off as memorized and robotic when used in interviews.

If you really want to get ahead in the media game and use the media to leverage your career potential, you need to go beyond the script. You need to form relationships with reporters and with your audiences.

During our first session, Brittney Griner really understood what I meant about forming relationships through her interview responses when I told her it was like "hugging people with words."

When people are done listening to an interview, they should want to embrace you in some way — as an athlete, as a person, as a role model, as an inspiration.

And in order to have that happen, you have to share a little bit about yourself — you have to go outside the script.

People don't get inspired by robotic, monotonous scripts.

People get inspired by real people, with real struggles, with real stories, with real successes. They get inspired by people who are unique and who add value to the teams they are on. They get inspired by people who make mistakes, but who learn from them. They get inspired by people who have stories, and who aren't afraid to share them.

Here are the three things you can do to hug people with words.

Let your personality shine

You are unique.

You've probably been told that since you were a child. But it's true! Don't strip the uniqueness out of yourself when you give an interview. Let some of your personality shine through.

I'm not saying ignore the team or organizational lines.

I AM saying add to them.

If one of your standard scripts is to thank your fans (which is a good policy) then add on a bit about why you like the fans so much. What cheer do they shout that makes you feel awesome? What touches you? Can you copy that cheer and give it back to the fans during your interview? If you feel comfortable doing that, then do it! Have some fun, and be yourself.

So many people get media coaching that puts them in a corner and makes them feel like they have to blend in and fit into a box. Not me. I avoid the box. That doesn't mean what's in the box doesn't have merit. It does. But that's not the whole package.

You bringing your personality to an interview completes the package—with a nice big bow. And when you let your personality shine through, people are more interested in the total package.

Story telling is captivating

For me, one of the best parts of kindergarten was story time. I loved listening to stories about animals and princesses and kings and beloved characters.

As an adult I love listening to people tell their stories about why they do what they do, and how they got to where they are in life.

When I listen to these stories, I find ways that I connect and identify with the storyteller. Ever have one of these connections? That is EXACTLY how you can hug people with words—by telling stories.

As I mentioned earlier, audiences are drawn to people with whom they can identify. If your story has something in common with a member of your audience and you share this story, you've made a connection. If you don't share this story, you miss out on an opportunity.

You don't have to have a long, drawn out story to share. That's not the point. Short, simple stories that give people a glimpse into your personality and into your life are important. It's easy to slip a short story into an interview.

> Reporter: What does it feel like to be drafted to play for Team XYZ?
>
> Athlete: When I was a kid I remember all I wanted for Christmas one year was a new bike. I wrote letters to Santa. I worked hard at behaving. And when I saw that bike on Christmas morning I couldn't imagine anything ever topping that. This is better than that! I'm so honored and excited to be joining the XYZ organization.

By sharing this short story, you tap into the emotions of your audience. You connect with anyone who ever wanted something special for Christmas. And you compare your current success with something they can identify with. This brings your audience closer to you, and makes you relatable.

Have a conversation

An interview is a conversation.

Plain and simple.

But so many people don't think of it that way. If you want to hug people with words, you have to have a conversation. You have to be yourself. You have to tell stories. And you have to do this in a conversational way.

An interview is a two-way street. The reporter may ask you a question to get it started, but you have the power to change the course of the interview through your answers.

Don't think of it as a simple Q & A session.

Think of the interview as an opportunity to share some of yourself, to get to know the reporter, and to find a good rhythm.

It's true — not all reporters are created equal and some are easier to talk to than others. But if you approach each reporter with the attitude of, "hey, let's talk and have a conversation about the game," instead of, "I have to answer a few questions about the game," you'll see great results.

Be open, be honest, be yourself, and be appropriate and respectful. If you follow those rules, you're likely on the road to media success.

YOUR GAME PLAN

- Share your **PERSONALITY** with people.
- Tell **STORIES** to connect to audiences.
- View interviews as a **CONVERSATION**.

Part 2:
Learning the Plays

You know that the media is important. You know that words can hurt. You know that your actions and words need to be consistent. And you know that building relationships by hugging people with words is what makes people connect to you.

Now it's time to learn some of the specifics that you can use to catapult your media presence to the next level. To use a sports analogy, you now understand the rules of the game. Now you're going to learn some plays that will lead you to victory.

Chapter 6

Pick-Up Lines: Interview responses that won't get you turned down

Let's cut to the chase. There are some pretty universal prerequisites when it comes to good interview etiquette. I'll give you these, and then I'll get into the nitty gritty — some specific responses to some very pointed questions.

Aside from being polite and courteous (and grateful for the chance to be interviewed — start looking at it that way instead of a hassle, and your attitude change will be visible to everyone) there are three standard things that you should do that make for a positive interview.

Thank your fans

Your fans are already on your side, so some athletes take them for granted. If you want to get in good with your support base, always make a point to thank them in your interviews.

Plus, it makes you appear gracious, kind, and appreciative.

Let's put this in a different perspective.

Some fans pay a significant amount of their income to come watch you and your team play. Shouldn't you recognize them for that effort?

Here are some lines that you can use.

> Reporter: Wow. What a close game. What do you have to say?
>
> Athlete: Well first I'd like to thank the fans. You guys stuck with us the whole way, and we really appreciate you backing us.
>
> ...or...
>
> First, our fans are incredible. We appreciate your support.
>
> ...or...
>
> We couldn't do it without our amazing fans. Thanks to all of you for coming out to support us today.

Acknowledge the other team

As much as it may frustrate you, especially if your team took a loss, it's important to recognize the other team and the players' efforts. This is being respectful and being "the bigger person" in the conversation.

You want to do this.

Your fans will admire you. The media will respect you. And you'll be putting off a good image of yourself and your organization.

I know it's not easy, but whatever you say, genuinely mean it. Here are some ways to incorporate your opponent into your response.

>Reporter: That was a tough loss.
>
>Athlete: It was. But I have to hand it to our opponents. They played hard.
>
>…or…
>
>Yeah. We never like to lose. But we lost to a great team.
>
>…or…
>
>Losses aren't fun. We played hard. But the other team got us in the end. All due respect to them. It was a good game.

You can also recognize and respect your opponent when you win.

>Reporter: You guys played a great game.
>
>Athlete: Thank you. We faced a very tough opponent and we had to really come together as a team to get this win.

Talk in "we" instead of "me"

Nobody likes an egomaniac. Before you go into an interview, check your ego at the door. The media is not a place for arrogance. At least not if you want to be viewed favorably and have a better chance at getting signed (or re-signed) and scoring more endorsements.

You've probably heard the saying, "There's no "I" in TEAM." So turn your "me" statements into "we" statements which acknowledge that you are a part of a greater whole — a part of a team.

Listen to how this sounds.

> Reporter: This was a tough game for you guys.
>
> Athlete: Yeah, I played as hard as I could but sometimes it isn't enough. My skills weren't at their best tonight. I normally play better. My fans didn't get to see that.

Sound a little self-absorbed? Here's how you can turn this "me" focus into a "we" response.

> Athlete: Yes it was. We worked hard but didn't get the outcome we would've liked. That happens sometimes. We're going to learn from this and do better next time.

Much better! Changing the pronouns makes a difference. Don't underestimate that.

YOUR GAME PLAN

- Be sure to **THANK FANS** in your responses.
- It's wise to **RECOGNIZE** your **OPPONENT** to show respect.
- Change your statements to **'WE' NOT 'ME'** statements.

Chapter 7

Trash Talk:
What NOT to say to a reporter

When you're exhausted and emotions are high sometimes it's easy for a reporter to get under your skin. But remember, you're in the spotlight. As much as you might want to throw a jab or say some choice words that would make your momma blush, don't.

Instead, try some of these techniques to avoid a sticky situation. You'll get asked questions that aren't as easy to respond to, but there are options for you. Here are some of those questions, and here are some responses that will be viewed positively.

First, breathe

If a reporter is approaching you as you're warming up, headed to the locker room, or immediately after a practice or game, you're already worked up. Your heart is pumping, the blood is flowing, and you're likely experiencing some type of natural high.

This is part of the addiction of sports.

But when all of these things are happening in your body, you need to remember to breathe.

Really breathe.

If someone is coming up to you and asking questions, take a breath before answering. Allow your body to take in oxygen and give your heart rate a chance to slow down.

It's important because it will not only help you slow your rate of speech, enunciate more clearly, and sound more collected, but it will also help calm any feelings of annoyance or frustration if a pressing question is asked.

Change the trajectory

Remember earlier when I mentioned an interview being a conversation? Well, if you're having a conversation with a friend and he brings up a topic you don't want to talk about, what do you do? Tell him you don't want to talk about it, or change the subject!

When a pointed question is thrown at you with the aim of getting a gut reaction, don't take the bait. Instead, redirect the conversation. Change the trajectory. Here are some examples of how to do it.

Reporter: It seems like after you threw that interception you lost all composure and went downhill from there. What happened?

Athlete: The other team played great defense. There's no denying that. We have work to do moving forward.

Here you acknowledge the other team and used "we" instead of "me," as you learned in the previous chapter. You also avoided taking the bait and danced around the subject. Not to mention you sound respectful in the process!

> Reporter: There are a lot of reports about you and your significant other publicly fighting. What's going on and how is it affecting your play?
>
> Athlete: Out of respect for my partner and our privacy I'd rather not talk about my personal life. I am, however, happy to discuss how our team is optimistic for the rest of the season and what new training we're doing to prepare us for the playoffs.

The boundaries of personal/private life are often obsolete in the media. But you do have the ability to change the trajectory of the conversation.

Use it respectfully, and you'll get great results.

Politely decline

You have the right to say "no comment." You have the right to not answer a question. It would be wise to use these options sparingly and with respect, but remember that you have power in each and every interview situation.

If a question is too personal, not relevant to the sport, or something that you know you cannot talk about without getting emotional, frustrated or angry, politely decline to answer.

Easier said than done? Maybe. But not after you read these options.

> Reporter: There are a lot of rumors circulating about a mid-season trade. What can you tell us about that?
>
> Athlete: I try not to get caught up in rumors. Let's talk about today's game instead.

Good work. By the first statement you let the reporter know that you realize what was asked, and then you generously offer up another topic of conversation.

If a reporter keeps harping on the original question, you aren't the one who will look bad.

Here's another example of how you may politely decline by addressing the question.

> Reporter: You guys looked like a different team out there today. Looks like (insert athlete's name here) being arrested had a big effect on the team.

Athlete: Any time you change team dynamics you're going to see a different performance. We didn't play the best game of the season. But we'll learn from our mistakes and move forward from here.

Again, you recognize that a question is being asked, but you skirt around it. And you sound great doing so. This is a good response.

Reporter: Your team is slated to win the championship this year. All of the major polls agree. What do you think about that?

Athlete: I think it's premature to talk about that right now. We are excited to start the season and hope to make our fans proud.

Great. You decline the topic right away in a respectful matter. You're integrating "we" into the answer and also your fans. This is a short, but sweet, response.

Remember, what happens in the locker room, stays in the locker room. Don't bring team politics into the media. Similarly, don't discuss disagreements with a coach or manager or teammate issues.

These are all situations where you need to be prepared to change the trajectory or politely decline.

Your Game Plan

- Don't forget to **BREATHE** before starting an interview.
- **CHANGE TRAJECTORY** if a question gets too personal.
- You can **POLITELY DECLINE** a question, but suggest another topic.

Chapter 8

Bad Breath:
What to do when reporters get too close or comfortable

The personal bubble. We all have one. For some it's smaller than others. But one thing is common, unless you're invited, you better not pop that bubble!

When it comes to interviewing in sports, sometimes you've got to get close. Too close. And potentially unpleasant or uncomfortable situations can present themselves.

Last year I spoke to a team about interview etiquette. A former MVP, no stranger to the media, asked:

> "What about when a reporter has bad breath? What should we do then?"

Immediately murmurs of recognition and a few bits of laughter echo through the room.

Let's face it. It's happened to all of us and we've all been approached by someone with it. Bad breath: What a mood killer!

This is just one issue that comes from a popping of the personal bubble. Other situations can include touching, intentional or accidental.

Here are three remedies for these bubble busters.

Body position

If the breath is really that bad, or the accidental touching is making you uncomfortable to the point that you can't hide your expression, position your body to the side instead of directly to the reporter.

I know this isn't ideal. But posturing towards the camera instead of to the reporter is a better option than making cringing facial expressions that will be recorded and replayed indefinitely.

If you do this, though, make sure that you put a lot of emphasis on the audience/fans in your responses. This way when you're looking more into the camera instead of at the reporter it'll be seen as you connecting (or wanting to connect) with the fans.

Posture perfect

Whenever you're giving an interview, make sure you stand-up or sit-up straight. Make sure your posture is natural to you.

You do not need to bend down to a reporter's height. He or she should raise the microphone for you or allow you to hold it yourself.

This should help with the bad breath issue, as well as personal distance.

But sometimes, especially if it's a pre-game, game, or post-game interview, it's really loud and hard to hear the question. So you have to bend down to hear.

With both the bad breath and personal space issues, you can make yourself a little more comfortable by tilting your head to the side slightly instead of bending directly to the reporter.

Side step

Another option, if there is an extra microphone and you have control over holding it, is to take a step back or to the side. This can easily be viewed as you wanting some air and not anything personal.

You can use this same technique if you have to share a microphone, but step to the side and look at the reporter, and step in only to answer the questions.

While the issue of bad breath may be a little comical, the issue of personal space is not. If you experience conduct that you feel is inappropriate or makes you uncomfortable, talk to the appropriate representative on your team, your agent, or your publicist.

YOUR GAME PLAN

- Angle your **BODY POSITION** to the side or slightly to the front or back.
- **POSTURE** yourself as you would in a regular conversation.
- You can **SIDE STEP** to get some space.

Chapter 9

Execution: Delivery matters

Now you understand the media landscape. You have some strategies for coping with tough questions. And you know the messages you need to send to get a positive reputation and repeat interviews.

Now it's time to execute with the final step: Delivery. In short, delivery matters.

Think back to the most boring speaker you've ever heard. Did he stand behind a podium and not move anywhere? Did she sound monotonous, like a robot? Did he speak so softly and with such a lack of enthusiasm that you wanted to fall asleep? Did she yell at the audience the entire time?

All of these examples are behaviors you want to avoid when you're giving an interview or giving any type of presentation on or off camera.

I'm going to give you three delivery tips that you can use to help make you sound more articulate, intelligent, and professional. They take practice.

But you're used to practice.

So just do it!

Enunciate and show your teeth

I know that heading probably throws you off some. That's okay. Let's break it down. When you enunciate, you are pronouncing each syllable in a word.

Remember back to elementary school when you had to hold your hand under your chin to count out how many syllables the word "macaroni" had? (The answer is four, by the way.) If you're enunciating words properly, you pronounce each syllable.

Another trick? It's nearly impossible to enunciate properly without showing a little glimpse of your pearly whites. Your teeth! When you enunciate you show your teeth. Think of the last person you saw lip sync well. It was realistic because you could see teeth throughout the performance. The mouth was open, pronouncing each word of the song and each syllable of each word, so you believed that she was singing.

Watch yourself speaking in a mirror. Do you mumble? Do you mutter? Do you not pronounce words completely? If any of these are true, they can all be fixed with proper enunciation. Open your mouth a little wider when you speak. It will slow your rate of speech, and make you easier to understand.

Paralanguage

What is paralanguage? Paralanguage is everything vocal other than words.

It's the rate (speed) at which you speak. It's the tone (volume) at which you project your voice. It's the pitch (highness or deepness) of your voice that comes out when you're excited or sad. It's what differentiates human speech from robotic speech. (Think of the phone voices on customer service lines, "For English, please press one.")

And an effective speaker will vary her rate, tone and pitch throughout a presentation or an interview. An effective speaker will let his emotional state show, without going overboard.

If you want to win over crowds and get reporters on your side, you need to use paralanguage effectively. If you're excited, it's okay to show it. You might not want to be jumping up and down and screaming like Tom Cruise on Oprah's couch (if you missed that, Google it), but it's okay to let out emotion. Just don't do it in an overly cocky or mocking way.

And how about giving a smile? Yes, men, you too. When you smile, your voice naturally changes and has variation. This is a good thing. You don't need to show your whole deck of teeth, but the corners of your mouth can turn up. You'd be surprised how well people receive you when you give off a bit of friendliness.

Likewise, it's okay to be disappointed. If you suffered a tough loss, or had a rough game, being happy wouldn't fit the message. It's okay to be more solemn. But you can be serious without being monotonous.

Listen to your past interviews. If they put you to sleep, you probably need to work on your paralanguage skills.

Avoid filler words

We talked a little bit about this in Chapter 3 when you reviewed a transcript with stuttering. Filler words are those "ums" and "uhs" "likes" and "you knows" that slip into your speech but don't add any real meaning to your message.

They take up unnecessary space, filling the gaps between one thought and another. Instead of filler words, try silence! A pause is a great strategic move. A pause gives you time to think and process. A pause makes you sound more intelligent than insignificant utterances.

Let's read this to make the point more clear.

With filler words:

> "Um I think we played good defense uh you know we have things to work on and uh we'll you know pull together and get even better."

Without filler words:

> "I think we played good defense. We have things to work on, but we'll pull together and get even better."

Convinced? I am.

Practice avoiding filler words and using pauses in your daily conversations. Have friends (who won't make too much fun of you) point out when you're using filler words. Listen to your past interviews and identify what phrases you say over and over again (such as, like, so, you know, etc.). The more you become aware of your behavior, the easier it is to change. It's really that simple. It just takes time and practice.

YOUR GAME PLAN

- **SHOW YOUR TEETH** a little bit to help enunciate your words.
- **VARY YOUR VOICE** to show a little emotion and make yourself human.
- **USE PAUSES** instead of using filler words.

Part 3:
Onward to Victory

You know what to say and how to say it. You understand the media landscape, and you've learned some valuable plays to help you stand out from the competition.

Now it's time to recognize that what you do outside of the interview, outside the limelight, matters in a big way. Let's talk about building community, and the always-present world of social media.

Chapter 10

Overtime:
Win after the interview and build community

Remember when we talked about sharing? Sharing builds relationships. Sharing builds community. But why do you need a community?

Simple. You can't do it alone.

You've made it to where you are because of a community. Your family and friends that supported you, your teammates who have your back, your coaches over the years who have helped you grow, and likely a large conglomerate of others.

As your community base grows, your value grows. The more followers you have (and I'm not just talking on Twitter) the more you are worth as a potential brand representative and the more you can earn for endorsements.

<u>Remember, your value is not just how you play the game, but what you bring to the game outside of your physical abilities</u>.

Here are three tips for adding value to your personal brand by building community.

Pick a cause, and advocate for it

You have the power to change your life, the lives of others, and your community for the better. You have the ability to affect, in a positive way, people you've never even met or never will meet. What an amazing feeling! But so many athletes don't leverage this.

Pick a cause that is near and dear to your heart, and advocate for it. Become a spokesperson for the cause. Volunteer for the cause. Donate money to the cause. And be open to talking about your support.

Share the story about what led you to support this particular cause. Let your community get to know you as a person, and not just a player.

Don't be a stranger: Be seen

An old adage says that it's better to be seen than heard. While this isn't always the case, being seen out in your community, making positive contributions, and being genuine and kind to others is a way to get people to see you as "one of them" and approachable.

This will lead to people wanting to support you more.

Don't get me wrong, I can understand how a routine trip to a restaurant can get derailed with people coming up to you and wanting a picture or autograph. I imagine that gets incredibly tiring.

But, if you can, take the time to do a few of these gestures of appreciation whenever you're out and about.

Your reputation as a "nice guy" or "great woman" will spread. And that will have snowballing effects.

> "But Jill," you may be thinking, "once I start doing this people keep coming and I can't get away. What do I do?"

Kindly tell people that you sincerely appreciate their enthusiasm and support, but that you would really like to focus on time with your close family and friends right now. People are generally understanding of that as long as you recognize their presence.

Publicly thank, recognize and encourage

Most people like to be recognized when they do well. I'm sure you like to know when you've broken a record, or played a good game, or made a friend happy. Your fans and supporters are no different.

If someone does something nice for you, publicly thank him. If someone goes out of her way to make a media appointment easy for you, recognize the effort. If someone tells you that you are a role model, encourage him to keep working hard.

But how do you do this publicly? You can use social media, and you can use your interviews!

If a fan did something really nice for you on the day of a game, or the week leading up to the game, and you can remember, thank that fan in your post-game interview. The reporter will love hearing an off-the-cuff story and that fan will remember you forever. Those stories make for easy sound-bites that reporters can run over and over again, and that media outlets can put on websites and on their social media channels. Doing a little good can go a long way.

Your Game Plan

- **PICK A CAUSE** and advocate — speak up.
- **BE SEEN** and be gracious out in your community.
- **PUBLICLY RECOGNIZE** outside of the norm efforts by fans and media.

Chapter 11

Death by Twitter:
Social media mistakes to avoid

Want Immortality?

Anything and everything you post on the Internet is immortal.

Period.

If there is a kryptonite to the average athlete it's the temptation of being too real, too available, and too open. As we talked about earlier—you are a public figure. Accept it. It's an honor, a responsibility and, sure, sometimes a pain in the butt.

But that's the reality.

This isn't to say that you can't be yourself, but you need to be the parts of yourself that brands and agencies will want to embrace.

You can't endorse a brand if you're tweeting or talking s*** left and right. Or, rather, you could, but you'll never be asked to.

Why? Brands want reliability. Brands want a solid investment. Brands want to stack the odds in their favor.

There are no point spreads that give you a break. Once a brand puts its money down on you, it plays to win. And a company will have no problem folding the hand if you do anything that is out of line or character with the brand that it's built.

And if you've used social media poorly in the past, you may have some cleaning up of your image to do.

Did you know that the United States Library of Congress archives tweets? It's true. Once you put something out via social media, it becomes permanent record.

Your 140 character musings, trash talk, Instagram snap shots, inappropriate or inside jokes…everything is out there for the world to consume not just now, but decades into the future.

Forget diamonds, tweets are forever.

So before you click "tweet" or "post" or "upload" or any other button that puts anything out into the virtual world, follow these guidelines to make sure that you want it to stick with you forever.

Family tree

Would you want your grandma or grandpa to read or see what you just posted? What about your mom or dad? Would you want your children or your children's children to see what you just Tweeted?

If the answer to any of these is "no" then stop immediately and delete whatever it is you were about to send into the virtual world.

There's no grey area here. Don't make a mistake that you can't take back.

Count to ten and click away

You can't control what others may tweet or post about you, but you can control how you respond. Do not get caught up in an argument online. No matter who it's with.

Anything you type or send can always get screen captured and posted out to the masses. Even if you think it's private. If someone is talking trash to you or about you, you can choose how you respond.

Not responding is a choice. (And is sometimes the better, wiser choice.)

When a nasty post comes up about you or your team or teammate online, don't do anything immediately. In fact, put your phone down, step away from the computer, or place the iPad in another room.

Don't type a response.

Count to ten, take a few breaths, and be rational about your response or click away from that site. People want to get a rise out of you. People want to get a response. Don't give them ammunition.

Of course, if you do respond, refer back to the "family tree" rule to make sure you really, really, want to click send.

A picture is worth a thousand words

Yes it's a cliché, but it's true. And this can be to your benefit or to your detriment. Let's get the negative out of the way first and cover what you should absolutely not be posting.

You should never, ever post pictures with a minor without direct, written consent from a parent or guardian. If you do, and if the picture is even slightly provocative, you could be under scrutiny for inappropriate behavior, child pornography or something worse. This happens to both male and female athletes, so beware.

Since pictures can be interpreted many ways, make sure anything you post can only be interpreted in a positive light. Sometimes it helps to run this by another person to make sure.

If you are doing an event and a young fan asks for a picture, that's okay. Don't be the one to post it without permission. Have that kid's parents post it if they want it out there (or have your agent work with them on a media release agreement).

Even though your behavior may be completely innocent, it just takes one minor misinterpretation to bring down a reputation.

I'm not trying to scare you. I'm trying to be real.

And, while it may seem obvious, I need to say it: No sexting! This is digital communication and can be retrieved even after it is deleted from your phone. Seriously.

You may not REALLY know how old a person is, and you could be setting yourself up for trouble without knowing it.

Don't send pictures or anything else that you wouldn't want family members to see. That family tree rule is the best one to always keep in mind.

On the plus side, if you're doing volunteer work and have a picture of yourself serving soup at a soup kitchen, building a home for less fortunate, coaching a children's clinic, do post these. Just make sure there are no minors in the picture (again, unless you have consent).

And talk about what you're doing.

Take pictures of the new pair of shoes you'll be rocking for your next game, the pre-game meal that you're having, or other day-to-day things that make you approachable and reachable.

This is a great way to endear yourself to the community and is a fun way for your fans to get to know you better, and for you to have a safe social media profile.

YOUR GAME PLAN

- Always think of the **FAMILY TREE** rule. What you post lasts forever.
- If someone tries to antagonize you, **COUNT TO TEN** before responding.
- Never, ever post **PICTURES** with a minor. Period.

Conclusion

Chapter 12

Beyond the Game: Your next steps

Congratulations!

You've navigated through ten chapters that gave you thirty game plans for media success.

Let's take a final look at your media playbook.

- The media can be your best friend, or your worst enemy. You have the power to turn the relationship either way. Use it for good, and the media can help you succeed beyond your wildest dreams.

- What you say, and how you say it, does matter. When you put something out there, it stays. So be aware of your surroundings and watch what comes out of your mouth. Use your words wisely, and you'll set yourself up for more opportunities.

- When your actions and your words don't match, people get confused (at best) and can think you're a hypocrite (at worst). Make sure that your message matches your behavior. Be consistent, and see results.

- Sharing your story and parts of yourself with fans and audiences is a way to hug people with words and get people to identify with and root for you. Giving a little bit of yourself can bring the masses to your side.

- Thanking your fans, acknowledging the other team and recognizing that you are a part of a team are all winning strategies that will keep you in the spotlight. Use these interview responses regularly, and sincerely, to see your media stock rise.

- If you're not comfortable answering a question, take a deep breath and either change the trajectory of the conversation or politely decline to answer. You have power in each and every interview. Be respectful, and you'll have no problem switching it up.

- Media is personal. But this doesn't mean that you need to have your personal space encroached upon. Use positioning strategies to make both you, and the reporter, more comfortable and you'll get more interviews.

- Taking the time to speak well pays off. Slow down, pronounce your words fully, and use pauses instead of filler words to give an all-star performance. If you're articulate and composed, reporters will come to you more, as they know they'll get a winning interview.

- Your media stock rises when you have a community behind you. Take time to build a base of supporters by being active where you live. Your fans will embrace you more, and the media will follow.

- Remember, what you put out on social media becomes permanent record. Hitting "delete" doesn't take your post or tweet away. Use social media wisely, and see amazing results.

My last piece of advice to you?

Take one game plan of one chapter at a time and work on it. Don't try to do everything at once.

When you first learned to play and compete in your chosen sport, you didn't become proficient with every aspect of the game in one practice. You won't with the media, either.

Just like you did (and do) with physical and strength training, you'll condition yourself over time to implement these media strategies until they become a natural part of your routine.

The crowd is cheering.

The odds are in your favor.

It's time to execute your new media strategies.

Game on!

Get Connected

Did reading this book help you gain confidence in your media skills? Did you knock out a killer interview using some of the tips provided in each chapter? Want to tell people about it and showcase your skills?

Let's connect!

Post your testimonials, feedback or even a link to your rock star interview to Impromptu Guru and share it with others.

 facebook.com/impromptuguru

 @impromptuguru

 youtube.com/impromptuguru

Tell your friends about this book.

http://theathletesmediaplaybook.com

About the Author

Jill Schiefelbein is an accomplished speaker, author, professor, and business owner. She is the owner of Impromptu Guru, a communication consulting company that was named Gilbert Arizona's 2012 "Rookie of the Year" less than a year after its inception. She works with professional athletes, politicians, business executives, and corporations to improve their communication, presentation and messaging strategies. In 2013, the WNBA's Phoenix Mercury named Impromptu Guru owner Jill Schiefelbein its official communication and media coach. She is also the host of "Communication Nation," a business communication talk show on VoiceAmerica's Business Channel that discusses how small changes in behavior can impact an organization's bottom line. In the higher education space, Schiefelbein is entering her tenth year teaching at Arizona State University, and regularly contributes to print and digital products about online education, communication and technology.

Learn more and view a full list of presentations and publications at http://impromptuguru.com.

Hire Jill

- Does your team need extra media training?
- Do you want to have a one-on-one session to really enhance your skills?
- Does your university want online media training options for its athletes?
- Do you want a keynote speaker to come to your next event to discuss communication and the media?
- Does your sales team need an extra push to get people in the seats?

Let's communicate!

Impromptu Guru offers one-on-one coaching, team and organization workshops, online course curricula, and virtual coaching services to athletes, universities and professional sports teams.

1-855-GO4-GURU

jill@impromptuguru.com

THANK YOU

Copyright © 2013 Impromptu Guru, LLC
All Rights Reserved.

www.ingramcontent.com/pod-product-compliance
Lightning Source LLC
LaVergne TN
LVHW051527070426
835507LV00023B/3349